True North

The NLP & Hypnotic Language Manifesting Planner - Create Your Own Destiny

Author: Kristen Becker

I0165724

True North

The NLP & Hypnotic Language Manifesting Planner - Create Your Own Destiny

Author: Kristen Becker

Published by Kristen Becker / Brillane LLC

ISBN: 978-0-578-37966-1

How to Use True North to Unlock Your Destiny & Make Your Manifesting Goals Inevitable

Be, Do, Have: What if there was a way to upgrade your beliefs quickly? There is a way, and you are holding it! This fantastic, life-changing tool will help you tap into the power of NLP and hypnotic language patterns to bring everything that matters most to you into manifestation permanently.

You have the creative power and control to create and live any life that you can imagine. No doubt, when you close your eyes and imagine, you probably have a clear idea of what that looks and feels like but are not sure how to bring it into your reality? This book is your key to unlocking your destiny!

You may have explored manifesting techniques and methods you've discovered along the way, only to find the same obstacles and roadblocks popping up over and over again. Here's why that happens. Your beliefs work much like the thermostat in your home. The temperature is set, and no matter how many doors or windows are opened, it will always maintain the temperature set on the thermostat. Likewise, your beliefs drive your reality. As within, so without! You can hustle, work, and visualize all you want; however, your outer world will always come into alignment with your inner beliefs. Your subconscious programming and the resulting habitual behavior & choices are all keeping your external world aligned with these inner beliefs.

This same process can also work to your advantage! As you update your beliefs, your programming, and automated habits all shift to align with them. You begin to naturally manifest everything that truly makes your soul feel alive and energized on autopilot! As within, so without!

There Is No Mystery!

In psychology & human behavior, the relationship between our beliefs and our reality is very well understood. Our beliefs, or subconscious programming, were installed when we were young, and our brains were in the alpha brainwave state. This is nature's way of helping us to be prepared to navigate life and live productively in our communities on autopilot (thanks nature!). As we get older, we start to realize that the true calling of our souls (our True North) is to expand far beyond those beliefs. We crave to live our lives in ways that inspire and uplift us. We feel the calling of a more fulfilling, meaningful, and passionate life. We realize that it's time to stop living from our installed programming and start living from our True North!

So How Do You Do That?

The way out is the same as the way in! In the same way, our beliefs and all the habits, choices, and behaviors that drive us on autopilot were created; we can also upgrade our beliefs, habits, choices, and behaviors to guide us on autopilot to our True North. Using the True North book daily allows you to rapidly & permanently upgrade your beliefs & habits and raise your vibration to align with your manifesting goal using NLP & powerful hypnotic language patterns!

Person A is the life that you are living now. Person A's life is driven on autopilot by the beliefs, choices, behaviors, etc., that were installed in childhood by those around you. These beliefs and associated habits were not created by you or serve your true desires, but they are driving your life for now.

Person B is the person who has already manifested all the dreams & life experiences that you KNOW to resonate with your soul. Person B shows up differently in the world & has an entirely different life experience! Person B has different beliefs, behaviors & habits than you have right now.

Person B is your True North! It's not that you must "become" anyone different to live the life you desire so deeply. It's simply that you need to remove the Person A programming & habit clutter to start living from your Person B True North. That is just what you are about to do. Get ready because living your life aligned with your True North is epic, empowering & amazing beyond even your wildest dreams!

My Destiny- 5-Year Vision at a Glance

Step 1: My Destiny- Define your overarching vision for your 5- year life goals for each area of life. It's your life. Dream BIG! What is your ideal state for each of these areas?

Step 2: Inside each smaller overlapping area, write in the one word that best describes your values, intentions, and goals for that area of your life. Research has shown that having a simple word to define your vision empowers you to embody the characteristics and habits that bring your goal to fruition.

Review your 5-year vision & intention words daily to keep yourself focused. Where your attention goes, your energy flows!

Note* for your 3-month True North goal, you will only be focusing on one manifesting goal. However, you will notice that all other areas in your life also transform right along with it because how you do one thing is how you do everything, and the beliefs that you are upgrading will filter into every area of your life.

My 3-Month Goal

Step 1: Define your 3-month manifesting goal. Don't hold back! You probably already know what you want and how it feels to have or experience it. Write out your 3-month goal in all its juicy & inspiring detail. Close your eyes and imagine your Person B and all the details of life with this manifesting goal realized. Focusing on one clearly defined goal is essential to ensure your success. You can include hard numbers where applicable, such as for vitality goals & business & finance goals. Be creative and explore specific markers that indicate the achievement of your goal.

A few goal examples for inspiration:
- Goal to find the perfect life partner: "My partner and I are spending high-quality time together at least three days per week, bonding and exploring life together."
- Goal to expand business: "I have identified and mastered the perfect marketing channel for you my business and am consistently doing 10k months."
- Goal to optimize health: "I am eating healthy, whole foods for 90% of my meals, exercising 3+ days per week, and am at my ideal weight of 137 pounds."

Step 2: Beliefs- Reflect on all the person A beliefs you have now that tell you what you want cannot be done, or you are not worthy of it, or the "evidence" of past patterns does not support it. Then reflect on Person B (your True North!). What do they believe, having already achieved these goals and living this life? What are the core beliefs that a person who has already achieved this goal has? Create a list of your person B beliefs. Fill in the beliefs section of your 3-month goal section with the three core beliefs that someone who has achieved this goal believes. For example, if your goal is to connect with a life partner, you might currently believe that "all of the good ones are taken, my chances are slim." In contrast, person B (who has already achieved this goal) might believe that the world is brimming with amazing single people and potential partners are everywhere. If your goal is to have 10k months in your business consistently, you may currently believe that "marketing is hard." While your person B belief might be that marketing is easy and just a numbers and testing game. If you have a health goal, you might currently hold the person A belief that "healthy foods are not as appealing." While the person B belief might be that healthy foods are far more delicious than processed foods.

Step 3: Belief Words- For each belief fill in one word that embodies and supports that belief. The words that we use are creating our subconscious programming day in and day out. Start infusing these words into your daily language & conversations both in your inner dialog/ self-talk and in discussions with others.

Step 4: Action Items- Looking at your primary goal and the beliefs that support it, break your goal down into the core nine action items that directly lead to achieving this goal. These action items will serve as your reference list when chunking down your monthly & weekly goals. Chunking a big goal down into smaller goals is a proven strategy to achieve any goal easily!

Review your 3-month goal daily. Always keep your face pointed in the direction you want to go!

Month At A Glance

There is no need to wait until the start of a calendar month to get started. The "month" is simply the next four weeks. Write in the dates to help keep track of your steps.

Step 1: Goal- Break your 3-month goal down into manageable chunks. What is the first and next logical step? Define your 1-month goal. You will build on and expand your goals accordingly for each consecutive month! You do not need to plan out all three monthly goals at this point, just the next logical step!

Step 2: Belief- Now, let's break those bigger belief patterns down into smaller chunks too. Looking at just your goal for the month, what is the "Person B" belief that you need to upgrade to manifest that goal? Fill in the belief you will upgrade this month.

Step 3: Mantra- Complete your "I am the kind of person who" statement that best supports your goals & belief upgrade for the month. Your "I am statement" is your power mantra for the month! You want to say this mantra daily throughout the month. Use it to set your intention at the start of your day, repeat it to yourself in your mind and work it onto your daily conversations.

Step 4: Action Items- What are the three most important actions you will commit to and accomplish this month to achieve your 1-month goal? Note that you will chunk your big action items into smaller steps each week.

Step 5: My Reward- Identify your monthly reward! It's vital to your success that you acknowledge your progress and celebrate your wins. Knowing each step moves you closer to your reward is highly motivating. Choose a reward that genuinely excites you- treat yourself! Each of your weekly goals leads you step-by-step to achieving your monthly goal. Check them off as you complete them each week, and then be sure to treat yourself to the reward at the end of the month and reflect on how it felt in the notes section of your month in review!

You WILL achieve what you focus on. Review your Month At A Glance daily!

Week At A Glance

Step 1: Goal- Write your weekly goal (a smaller chunk of the monthly goal) that you will focus on this week to move you closer to your goal. Be sure to check it off once you have achieved it to move closer to your monthly goal reward!

Step 2: Belief- Write the belief that you are upgrading this week. You want to focus on just one belief to boost each week so you can make progress on that belief. Choose the belief that most directly relates to & supports your weekly goal.

Step 3: Action Items- As the saying goes, "if you have more than three priorities, you have none." Write in the three core items that you will accomplish this week that accomplish your weekly goal. You will chunk each one into smaller action items for your daily planning each week.

Step 4: Mantra- Complete the "I am the kind of person who" statement that sets your intention & supports your goals & belief upgrades for the week. Repeat this mantra all week long & work the main idea into your conversations & self-talk.

Step 5: Vibe Check- Circle the icon that best describes where you are on the manifesting scale about your True North 3-month goal & beliefs. Knowing exactly where you are, empowers you to identify what comes next and where you are going. It's gratifying to see yourself move up the scale month after month!

Review the next two pages for The Manifesting & Scale & how to use it!

Manifesting Scale

Frequency	Qualities	
700+	Enlightenment	Enlightenment
600+	Synchronicity	Peace/Joy
500	Extra-Ordinary Outcomes	Love
350	Peak Performance Without Stress	Acceptance
310	Peak Performance Without Stress	Willingness
250	Productive	Neutrality
200	Hyperactivity	Pride/Courage
100	Hyperactivity	Fear/Anger
0	Inaction	Shame/Guilt

KRISTEN
BECKER

How To Use The Manifesting Scale

- **Frequency:** The vibrational frequency associated with each emotion & quality.
- **Qualities:** The nature of your state & how you navigate the nuances of life at each phase of the scale.
- **Emotions:** The feelings & emotions that identify the nature of your current state. We tend to travel the emotional scale in order.

The manifesting scale is based on the scale of consciousness by Dr. David Hawkins, the scale of emotions, and the corresponding scale of behavioral characteristics. Being aware of your vibrational state is the first step in raising it. Knowing your options and what to expect when you choose to go in any direction is the next step.

Knowing where you are at any point in time, on any given area in your life on the vibrational scale, is vital to moving yourself up the scale. However, just looking at it in terms of vibration can sometimes seem esoteric & more challenging to use. However, our emotions are synonymous with vibrational frequencies and reflected in our current circumstances and the qualities of our life. Looking at the big picture in this way makes it easy to know exactly where you are on the scale and what to do next!

As you assess your current state, beliefs, & choices related to your goals, frequently refer to the manifesting scale. Take an honest assessment of where you are on the scale and notice what comes next. You will get inspired ideas about what beliefs you are ready to upgrade and what types of behaviors & choices to focus on to move up to the next level! It clarifies what kinds of emotions you will travel through next to move up the scale. For example, if you are currently angry about a circumstance, you can expect to take pride in your right to live your life on your terms and then lean into the courage to take the following steps to move you into your desired state. It also empowers you to become aware of where you are and how far you have traveled up the scale as you move through the achievement process. Referring to the Manifesting Scale will inspire and empower you and serve as a measurement tool to celebrate your wins!

The emotions on the manifesting scale read from left to right, going from the lowest to the higher feelings in each section. For example, the order from lowest to most heightened vibrating emotions on the bottom of the scale is shame, guilt, apathy, grief, fear.

- Refer to the manifesting scale daily to assess where you are, where you want to be, and what steps to take next.
- Refer to the scale at the start of each week to assess your progress toward your goal & your True North!

Daily Prompts

Step 1: Morning- Action Items- Fill in your action items for the day. These should all be things that lead directly to the achievement of your weekly goal.

Step 2: Evening- Complete the "The More I, The More I" & "The Less I, The Less I" sections. This process uses cause & effect to connect your new choices with your desired results & quickly upgrades your subconscious programming to support your goal. For example, if you are working on a vitality goal and your action item for the day was eating whole foods and the belief you are upgrading for the week is that healthy foods are delicious and satisfying, your statements might look something like this:

- "The more I learn about how to prepare healthy foods, the more I realize how truly delicious they are."
- The more whole foods I eat, the more energy and creative spark I have."
- "The more whole foods I eat, the less I can stand the taste of processed foods."
- "The less I eat junk food, the less I crave junk food."

Again, this is a decisive step in the process as it makes you aware of the cause and effect and quickly upgrades your subconscious programming to align with your goals. You can think of this sort of as a daily gratitude journal for your new habits & beliefs.

Step 4: Weekly Notes Area- use the notes area at the end of each week for reminders, inspirations, or anything that helps you.

Month In Review

It's time to do the "Monday morning quarterbacking" and take stock of what worked (and why) and what did not work, and how it inspires you moving forward.

Step 1: Wins & Gains- Identify three ways you grew & made progress. Focusing on the evidence of your progress builds belief quickly and raises your vibration.

Step 2: Learns & Insights- There are no mistakes, only opportunities to get more clarity. Identify three ways in which you became more precise on what you want, what you don't want, what works, what doesn't work, and so on. This valuable insight will empower you to make laser-focused, True North centered choices for yourself moving forward.

Step 3: Celebrate- Confidence is key to success & living your True North. Practice makes permanent. The more you do something, the more confident you become in that area. Take note of the specific ways, places, and areas in which you become more confident this month.

Treat yourself to the reward you set up for the month and be sure to write about how it felt to enjoy that reward in the notes area!

It's Time to Live Your True North & Create Your Own Destiny. Your Journey Begins Now!

My Destiny

5 Year Vision at a Glace

Vitality

Relationships

Career

Self-expression

Outer: Goals | **Inner:** Intention words

My True North

3 Month Goal

BELIEFS

BELIEF WORDS

ACTION ITEMS

1	1	1
2	2	2
3	3	3

My True North
Month at a Glance

1 - Month Goal

Belief

Mantra: I am the kind of person who:

Action Items

1 _____

2 _____

3 _____

⭐ My Reward:

Week at a Glance   Date: /   /

☆ **Goal:**

Belief:

☆ Action item 1:

☆ Action item 2:

☆ Action item 3:

Mantra: I am the kind of person who:

Vibe Check - Circle your vibe status

Action Items   **Day/Date:**

1

2

3

The More I / The More I & The Less I / The Less I:

Action Items   **Day/Date:**

1

2

3

The More I / The More I & The Less I / The Less I:

Action Items   Day/Date:

1

2

3

The More I / The More I & The Less I / The Less I:

Action Items   Day/Date:

1

2

3

The More I / The More I & The Less I / The Less I:

Action Items

Day/Date:

1

2

3

The More I / The More I & The Less I / The Less I:

Action Items

Day/Date:

1

2

3

The More I / The More I & The Less I / The Less I:

Action Items

Day/Date:

1

2

3

The More I / The More I & The Less I / The Less I:

Weekly Notes

Week at a Glance   Date: /   /

☆ Goal:

Belief:

☆ Action item 1:

☆ Action item 2:

☆ Action item 3:

Mantra: I am the kind of person who:

Vibe Check - Circle your vibe status

Action Items   **Day/Date:**

1

2

3

The More I / The More I & The Less I / The Less I:

Action Items   **Day/Date:**

1

2

3

The More I / The More I & The Less I / The Less I:

Action Items   **Day/Date:**

1

2

3

The More I / The More I & The Less I / The Less I:

Action Items   **Day/Date:**

1

2

3

The More I / The More I & The Less I / The Less I:

Action Items   Day/Date:

1

2

3

The More I / The More I & The Less I / The Less I:

Action Items   Day/Date:

1

2

3

The More I / The More I & The Less I / The Less I:

Action Items   Day/Date:

1

2

3

The More I / The More I & The Less I / The Less I:

Weekly Notes

Week at a Glance

Date: / /

☆ Goal:

Belief:

☆ Action item 1:

☆ Action item 2:

☆ Action item 3:

Mantra: I am the kind of person who:

Vibe Check - Circle your vibe status

Action Items

Day/Date:

1

2

3

The More I / The More I & The Less I / The Less I:

Action Items

Day/Date:

1

2

3

The More I / The More I & The Less I / The Less I:

Action Items

Day/Date:

1

2

3

The More I / The More I & The Less I / The Less I:

Action Items

Day/Date:

1

2

3

The More I / The More I & The Less I / The Less I:

Action Items   **Day/Date:**

1

2

3

The More I / The More I & The Less I / The Less I:

Action Items   **Day/Date:**

1

2

3

The More I / The More I & The Less I / The Less I:

Action Items

1

2

3

The More I / The More I & The Less I / The Less I:

Weekly Notes

Week at a Glance   Date: /   /

⭐ Goal:

Belief:

☆ Action item 1:

☆ Action item 2:

☆ Action item 3:

Mantra: I am the kind of person who:

Vibe Check - Circle your vibe status

Action Items   **Day/Date:**

1

2

3

The More I / The More I & The Less I / The Less I:

Action Items   **Day/Date:**

1

2

3

The More I / The More I & The Less I / The Less I:

Action Items

Day/Date:

1

2

3

The More I / The More I & The Less I / The Less I:

Action Items

Day/Date:

1

2

3

The More I / The More I & The Less I / The Less I:

Action Items

Day/Date:

1

2

3

The More I / The More I & The Less I / The Less I:

Action Items

Day/Date:

1

2

3

The More I / The More I & The Less I / The Less I:

Action Items   Day/Date:

1

2

3

The More I / The More I & The Less I / The Less I:

Weekly Notes

Month in Review

⭐ I achieved my goal

Wins & Gains - Ways I grew!

1 _____

_____

2 _____

_____

3 _____

_____

Learns & Insights: How I got more clarity!

1 _____

_____

2 _____

_____

3 _____

_____

Celebrate - I am now much more confident about/at/in:

notes _____

_____

_____

_____

My True North

Month at a Glance

1 - Month Goal

Belief

Mantra: I am the kind of person who:

Action Items

1 _____
_____
_____

2 _____
_____
_____

3 _____
_____
_____

☆ **My Reward:**

Week at a Glance   Date: /   /

☆ Goal:

Belief:

☆ Action item 1:

☆ Action item 2:

☆ Action item 3:

Mantra: I am the kind of person who:

Vibe Check - Circle your vibe status

Action Items   Day/Date:

1

2

3

The More I / The More I & The Less I / The Less I:

Action Items   Day/Date:

1

2

3

The More I / The More I & The Less I / The Less I:

Action Items   Day/Date:

1

2

3

The More I / The More I & The Less I / The Less I:

Action Items   Day/Date:

1

2

3

The More I / The More I & The Less I / The Less I:

Action Items   Day/Date:

1

2

3

The More I / The More I & The Less I / The Less I:

Action Items   Day/Date:

1

2

3

The More I / The More I & The Less I / The Less I:

Action Items

Day/Date:

1

2

3

The More I / The More I & The Less I / The Less I:

Weekly Notes

Week at a Glance   Date: /   /

⭐ **Goal:**

Belief:

☆ Action item 1:

☆ Action item 2:

☆ Action item 3:

Mantra: I am the kind of person who:

Vibe Check - Circle your vibe status

Action Items

Day/Date:

1

2

3

The More I / The More I & The Less I / The Less I:

Action Items

Day/Date:

1

2

3

The More I / The More I & The Less I / The Less I:

Action Items   **Day/Date:**

1

2

3

The More I / The More I & The Less I / The Less I:

Action Items   **Day/Date:**

1

2

3

The More I / The More I & The Less I / The Less I:

Action Items

Day/Date:

1

2

3

The More I / The More I & The Less I / The Less I:

Action Items

Day/Date:

1

2

3

The More I / The More I & The Less I / The Less I:

Action Items   Day/Date:

1

2

3

The More I / The More I & The Less I / The Less I:

Weekly Notes

Week at a Glance   Date: / /

☆ Goal:

Belief:

☆ Action item 1:

☆ Action item 2:

☆ Action item 3:

Mantra: I am the kind of person who:

Vibe Check - Circle your vibe status

Action Items   **Day/Date:**

1

2

3

The More I / The More I & The Less I / The Less I:

Action Items   **Day/Date:**

1

2

3

The More I / The More I & The Less I / The Less I:

Action Items

Day/Date:

1

2

3

The More I / The More I & The Less I / The Less I:

Action Items

Day/Date:

1

2

3

The More I / The More I & The Less I / The Less I:

Action Items   Day/Date:

1

2

3

The More I / The More I & The Less I / The Less I:

Action Items   Day/Date:

1

2

3

The More I / The More I & The Less I / The Less I:

Action Items

1

2

3

The More I / The More I & The Less I / The Less I:

Weekly Notes

Week at a Glance   Date: /   /

☆ Goal:

Belief:

☆ Action item 1:

☆ Action item 2:

☆ Action item 3:

Mantra: I am the kind of person who:

Vibe Check - Circle your vibe status

Action Items   Day/Date:

1

2

3

The More I / The More I & The Less I / The Less I:

Action Items   Day/Date:

1

2

3

The More I / The More I & The Less I / The Less I:

Action Items   Day/Date:

1

2

3

The More I / The More I & The Less I / The Less I:

Action Items   Day/Date:

1

2

3

The More I / The More I & The Less I / The Less I:

Action Items

Day/Date:

1

2

3

The More I / The More I & The Less I / The Less I:

Action Items

Day/Date:

1

2

3

The More I / The More I & The Less I / The Less I:

Action Items   **Day/Date:**

1

2

3

The More I / The More I & The Less I / The Less I:

Weekly Notes

Month in Review

⭐ I achieved my goal

Wins & Gains - Ways I grew!

1 _____
_____

2 _____
_____

3 _____
_____

Learns & Insights: How I got more clarity!

1 _____
_____

2 _____
_____

3 _____
_____

Celebrate - I am now much more confident about/at/in:

---

notes _____
_____
_____
_____

My True North

Month at a Glance

1 - Month Goal

Belief

Mantra: I am the kind of person who:

Action Items

1 _____
_____
_____

2 _____
_____
_____

3 _____
_____
_____

☆ My Reward:

Week at a Glance   Date: /   /

⭐ Goal:

Belief:

☆ Action item 1:

☆ Action item 2:

☆ Action item 3:

Mantra: I am the kind of person who:

Vibe Check - Circle your vibe status

Action Items   **Day/Date:**

1

2

3

The More I / The More I & The Less I / The Less I:

Action Items   **Day/Date:**

1

2

3

The More I / The More I & The Less I / The Less I:

Action Items

Day/Date:

1

2

3

The More I / The More I & The Less I / The Less I:

Action Items

Day/Date:

1

2

3

The More I / The More I & The Less I / The Less I:

Action Items

Day/Date:

1

2

3

The More I / The More I & The Less I / The Less I:

Action Items

Day/Date:

1

2

3

The More I / The More I & The Less I / The Less I:

Action Items

1

2

3

The More I / The More I & The Less I / The Less I:

Weekly Notes

Week at a Glance   Date: /   /

☆ Goal:

Belief:

☆ Action item 1:

☆ Action item 2:

☆ Action item 3:

Mantra: I am the kind of person who:

Vibe Check - Circle your vibe status

Action Items	Day/Date:
1	
2	
3	

The More I / The More I & The Less I / The Less I:

Action Items	Day/Date:
1	
2	
3	

The More I / The More I & The Less I / The Less I:

Action Items   Day/Date:

1

2

3

The More I / The More I & The Less I / The Less I:

Action Items   Day/Date:

1

2

3

The More I / The More I & The Less I / The Less I:

Action Items

Day/Date:

1

2

3

The More I / The More I & The Less I / The Less I:

Action Items

Day/Date:

1

2

3

The More I / The More I & The Less I / The Less I:

Action Items

Day/Date:

1

2

3

The More I / The More I & The Less I / The Less I:

Weekly Notes

Week at a Glance   Date: /   /

☆ **Goal:**

Belief:

☆ Action item 1:

☆ Action item 2:

☆ Action item 3:

Mantra: I am the kind of person who:

Vibe Check - Circle your vibe status

Action Items	Day/Date:

1

2

3

The More I / The More I & The Less I / The Less I:

Action Items	Day/Date:

1

2

3

The More I / The More I & The Less I / The Less I:

Action Items   Day/Date:

1

2

3

The More I / The More I & The Less I / The Less I:

Action Items   Day/Date:

1

2

3

The More I / The More I & The Less I / The Less I:

Action Items   **Day/Date:**

1

2

3

The More I / The More I & The Less I / The Less I:

Action Items   **Day/Date:**

1

2

3

The More I / The More I & The Less I / The Less I:

Action Items

Day/Date:

1

2

3

The More I / The More I & The Less I / The Less I:

Weekly Notes

Week at a Glance   Date: /   /

⭐ Goal:

Belief:

☆ Action item 1:

☆ Action item 2:

☆ Action item 3:

Mantra: I am the kind of person who:

Vibe Check - Circle your vibe status

Action Items

Day/Date:

1

2

3

The More I / The More I & The Less I / The Less I:

Action Items

Day/Date:

1

2

3

The More I / The More I & The Less I / The Less I:

Action Items   **Day/Date:**

1

2

3

The More I / The More I & The Less I / The Less I:

Action Items   **Day/Date:**

1

2

3

The More I / The More I & The Less I / The Less I:

Action Items   **Day/Date:**

1

2

3

The More I / The More I & The Less I / The Less I:

Action Items   **Day/Date:**

1

2

3

The More I / The More I & The Less I / The Less I:

Action Items

1

2

3

The More I / The More I & The Less I / The Less I:

Weekly Notes

Month in Review

⭐ I achieved my goal

Wins & Gains - Ways I grew!

1 _____

_____

2 _____

_____

3 _____

_____

Learns & Insights: How I got more clarity!

1 _____

_____

2 _____

_____

3 _____

_____

Celebrate - I am now much more confident about/at/in:

notes _____

_____

_____

Congratulations! You are a beautiful and intelligent individual who deserves to live life on your terms. I'm so proud of the journey you are taking and the investment you have made in yourself by completing your three-month goal!

I invite you to reflect on the transformation that you have created for yourself over the past three months. What a beautiful gift you have given yourself. You have taken back control of your destiny and designed the life you want to live!

When you invest in yourself, momentum builds exponentially. The more focus and energy you put into your life, the better it becomes as a whole; this begins to happen faster with each passing day as the whole process starts to become mental muscle memory and occurs on autopilot.

Keep your momentum going. Order your next planner today!

Brainstorm- Ideas for my next few goals:

Notes

www.ingramcontent.com/pod-product-compliance
Lightning Source LLC
Chambersburg PA
CBHW080536090426
42733CB00015B/2598